Little Life Savers at Home

Acknowledgements

I will be eternally grateful to Joan and the good folks at Tangerine Publications for encouraging me to share this book with the world.

I would also like to thank Iain for endless support, Mum and Dad for nurturing the 'little life saver' in me, Ben and Max for the inspiration and Peter Gallagher of the New Zealand Fire Service for generously sharing time and advice.

Little Life Savers at Home

Written by Stella McCallum
Illustrated by Alan and Dennis Poole

Introduction

Teaching your child how to stay safe in an emergency might be one of the most valuable lessons you ever share with them. I have written this book because most safety education for children is aimed at those of school age. There is very little guidance for parents and other educators who want to teach their children about safety at an earlier age, yet we hear news stories of little heroes aged three or four saving the lives of their parents or caregivers in an emergency. In fact, each year, hundreds of young children around the world save lives by contacting emergency services when a parent, grandparent, sibling, or babysitter collapses. Heart attacks and strokes require urgent medical attention and, however unpleasant it might be to imagine, it is quite possible that such an emergency may occur in the presence of your child.

This book also presents two other emergencies that may occur in the home. Safety information regarding fire and earthquakes is unique to each emergency situation and it's important that young children learn the appropriate response in each event and understand that saving their own lives is of paramount importance and equally as heroic as saving the lives of others.

This book has been designed to empower our Little Life Savers and assist in the development of valuable safety skills. The information is presented to your child in a simple and non-threatening manner, using plain language and appealing characters.

At the end of the picture book section of this resource, you will find some tips and examples of things you could discuss with your child. I suggest that you familiarise yourself with this section before you begin reading the picture book with your child.

Stella McCallum

Lucy and Sam are Little Life Savers.

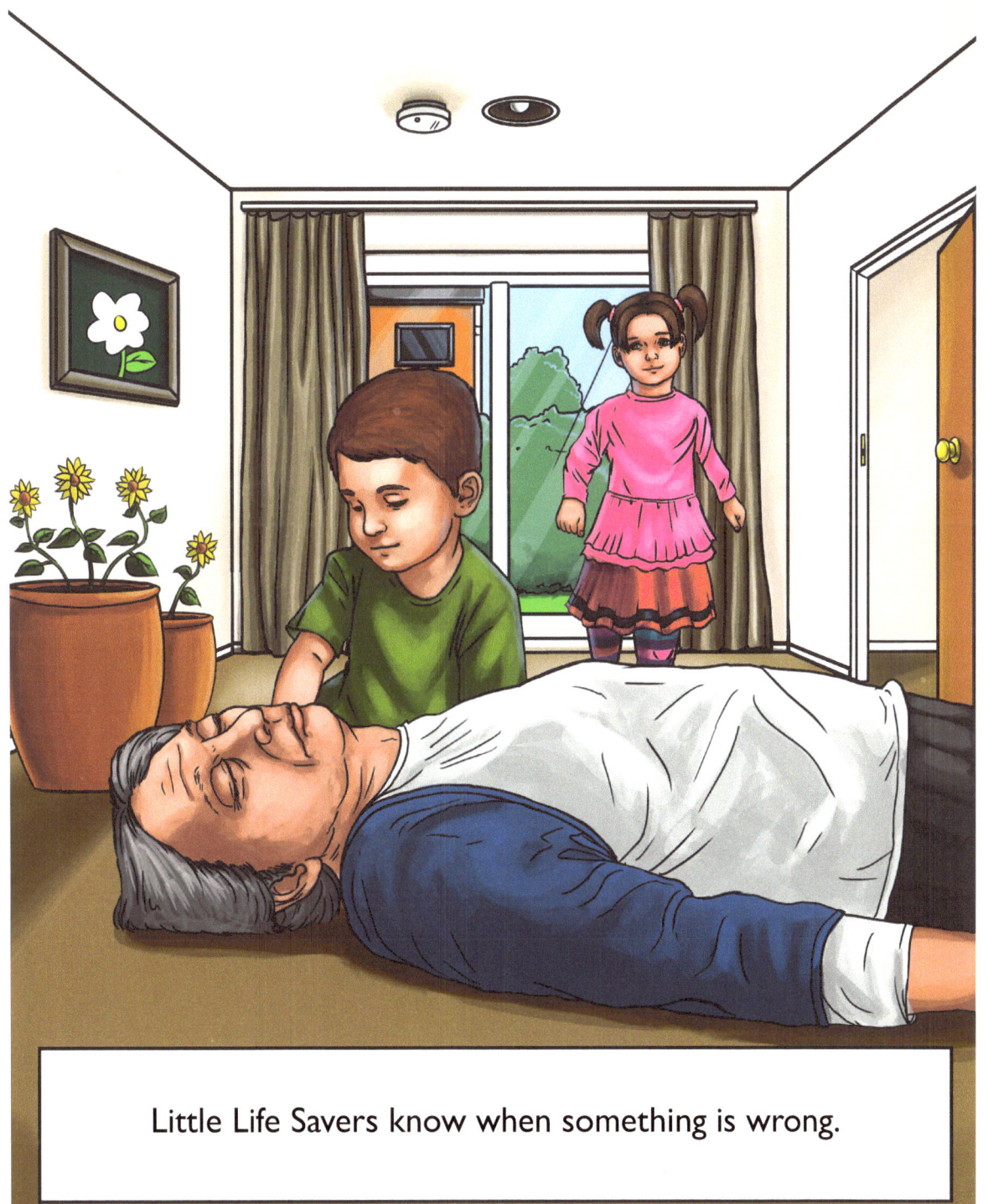

Little Life Savers know when something is wrong.

Little Life Savers can reach the phone.

Sam knows how to dial 111.

This Little Life Saver knows her address.

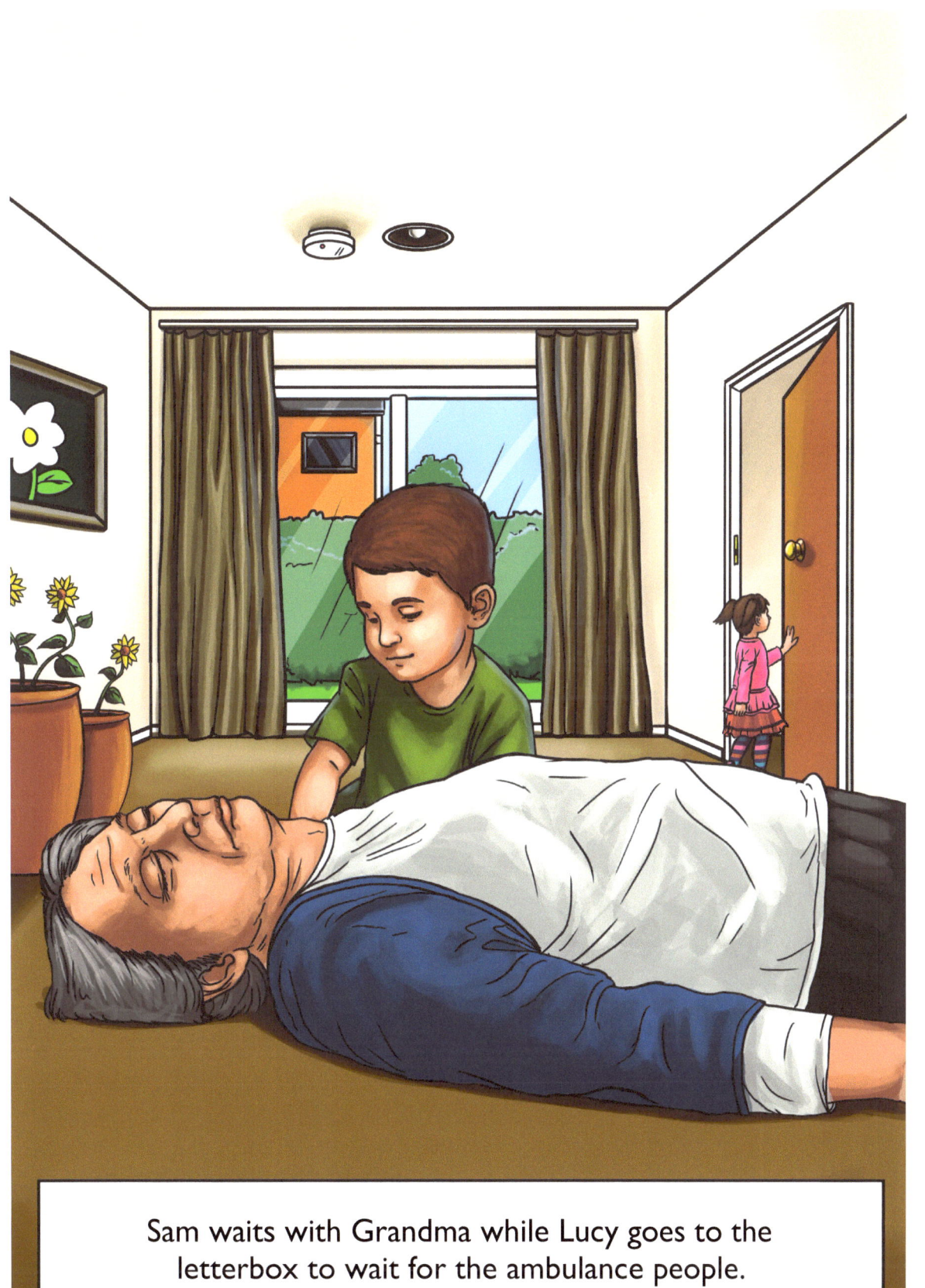

Sam waits with Grandma while Lucy goes to the letterbox to wait for the ambulance people.

At the letterbox, Lucy meets Mrs Kindly.

Sam knows he's not allowed to touch the first-aid box, but he knows where it is.

The ambulance people take care of Grandma.

Little Life Savers practise fire drills. The smoke alarm makes a loud noise, but it does not frighten Lucy and Sam. Little Life Savers don't run and hide.

Sam knows what to do when there is a real fire.

Lucy knows what to do when there is a real fire.

Sam and Lucy know lots of ways to get out of their house.

Little Life Savers know a safe place to wait for help.

Sam can feel an earthquake.

Lucy knows there is an earthquake.

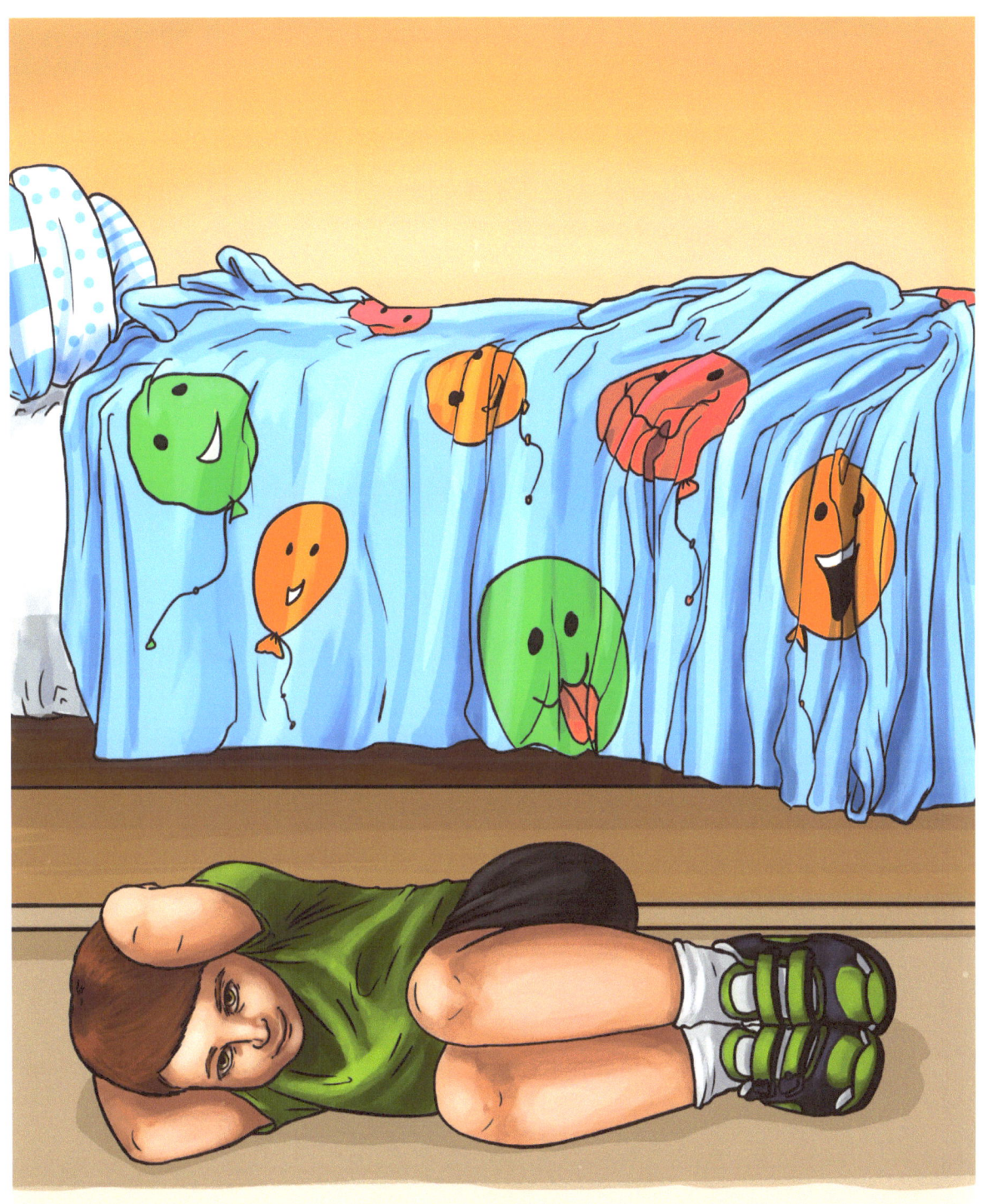

Little Life Savers know how to find a safe place during an earthquake.

Mum and Dad know they are safe.

Guidance for Parents, Caregivers and Teachers

Page 1 – 'Lucy and Sam are Little Life Savers'

Could your child be a Little Life Saver? No one likes to imagine that these skills may ever be required of a child, but accidents and illnesses happen. It's never too early to introduce your child to some of the principles of safety and emergency response. These lessons should be undertaken in a non-threatening way, as it is not pleasant for a young child to imagine that he or she may be required to act independently in an emergency situation. However, to signify the importance of the information, you should try to avoid jokes.

Suggested questions

- *What do you think a Little Life Saver is?*
- *Shall we learn about how you could become a Little Life Saver?*

Page 2 – 'Lucy and Sam know when something is wrong'

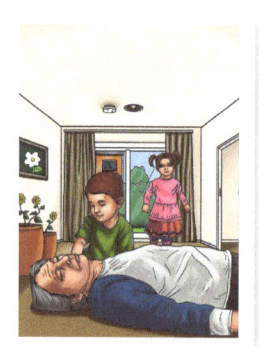

Children must be able to identify a real emergency. You could discuss different emergency situations with your child, such as falling down the stairs, choking, falling to the ground, or your child's inability to wake someone. The child should learn that fights with siblings, lost treasures and unwelcome discipline are not grounds to alert the emergency services.

Suggested questions

- *What do you think the word emergency means?*
- *Who helps us in an emergency?*
- *What would you do if you couldn't wake Grandma/Grandpa?*
- *What should you do if you lose your favourite toy?*
- *What should you do if your brother/sister is being mean to you?*

Page 3 – 'Little Life Savers can reach the phone'

Recent statistics from New Zealand police, fire and ambulance services indicate that approximately 330,000 emergency '111' calls are placed each year, but only 12,000 require an emergency response. Calling for help is the most important thing a child can do in an emergency, but due to valid concerns about the improper use of the phone, adults may be tempted to keep the phone out of reach of little children. This could potentially be dangerous in an emergency. Instead, it might be wise to advise your child about the importance of correct use and the consequences of inappropriate calls. Your child should never regard the phone as a toy or be given the home phone or a mobile phone to play with. However, under your supervision, your child could familiarise him/herself with the keypad when the phone is disconnected.

Suggested questions

- *Where do we keep the phone in this house?*
- *Are there any other phones you could use if there was an emergency?*
- *Can you name some places we might keep a mobile phone?*
- *What would you do if you needed to make a call on our home phone and you couldn't find it? (If appropriate: Do you know which button you push to locate the phone handset?)*
- *Why should we never play with the phone?*

Page 4 – 'Little Life Savers know how to dial 111'

You cannot take for granted your child's knowledge of the number or assume that your child is too young to learn it. If your child can communicate verbally, he or she is old enough to dial '111'. When teaching children how to use '111', you must emphasise that the number is for emergency use only. To avoid panicking and forgetting the numbers, you could display '111' in bold print by the telephone. You may also want to teach your child how to use a mobile phone, as there may be some operational differences.

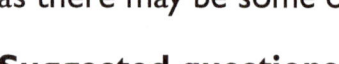
Sam knows how to dial 111

Suggested questions

- *What number do we call in an emergency?*
- *Who might be sent to help us if we dial 111?*
- *Do you know how to dial 111?*
- *Who should you call if there is a fire?*
- *Who should you call if someone is very sick?*
- *Why should we never call this number when there is no real emergency?*

Page 5 – 'This Little Life Saver knows his full name' and Page 6 – 'This Little Life Saver knows her address'

You should make sure that your child knows his or her full name and address. As emergency service calls are regularly answered out-of-town and street names are often duplicated in different towns, it is important that knowledge of your child's address should include the town name. You can practise this through role-play and, when you and your child are walking around the neighbourhood, by identifying street names, house numbers and landmarks. Labelling your child's possessions with full name and address and telephone numbers will provide regular exposure to the information and help your child remember it.

You might like to role-play an emergency call situation with your child and this will help you to assess the level of preparedness for the operator's questions.

Suggested questions

- *Can you tell me your full name?*
- *Do you know what a surname is?*
- *Can you tell me your address?*
- *What town/city do we live in?*

Page 7 - 'Don't hang up until you're told to'

Call tracing has become more efficient and if 'Caller ID' is activated, your child may only have to stay connected to the emergency services operator for 25-30 seconds in order to be located, or one minute if 'Caller ID' is de-activated. However, you should advise your child to stay on the line until instructed by the operator to hang up so that helpful information is relayed. It may be important to emphasise that the person answering the emergency is a stranger who your child can trust with personal information. Emergency call operators are trained to assist callers and should provide your child with some reassurance of their actions and the situation.

In addition to simple questions regarding name, address and phone number, some of the questions asked by operators that may pose more difficulty for your child are, for example, 'Which emergency service do you require?' 'What is the nature of the emergency?' 'Is the person conscious?' 'What is the exact location of the emergency?' 'Can you stay on the line?' 'Where is the closest cross-street/nearest intersection?' You might like to extend the role-play to introduce more difficult questions once your child has responded appropriately to basic questions.

Suggested questions

- *Who answers 111 calls?*
- *Can we trust this stranger?*
- *Is it okay to tell the operator embarrassing things?*
- *Why should we stay on the phone until the operator tells us to hang up?*
- *Why do you think the operator needs to ask so many questions?*
- *Can you think of some of the questions the operator might ask?*
- *What might happen if you hang up the phone before the operator says it's okay?*

Page 8 – 'Sam waits with Grandma while Lucy goes to the letterbox'

In the event that a caregiver becomes unresponsive due to ill health or an accident, a child may feel distressed and powerless to help. However, prompt action is vital for the safety of the caregiver and the unsupervised child. Discussing some potential scenarios in a non-threatening manner, within the child's scope of comprehension, could empower and enable the child to act safely, get help and reduce any feelings of anxiety. You could also prepare your child for the possibility that a different emergency service may arrive before the one that your child was expecting. Due to excessive demand on a certain service at any given time, your child could be concerned about the arrival of a fire engine when expecting an ambulance.

With your child, you should agree on a safe meeting spot to wait for help in the event of any emergency. For more details on the selection of a safe meeting spot, please see guidance for page 16.

Suggested questions

- *Why do you think Sam chose to stay with Grandma?*
- *Why do you think Lucy chose to go to the letterbox?*
- *What would you do after you called 111, if you were alone?*
- *What would you do after you called 111, if you were with a brother/sister/friend?*
- *Do you think it's okay for a policeman to turn up if you called for an ambulance?*
- *Why do you think that might happen?*

Page 9 – 'At the letterbox, Lucy meets Mrs Kindly'

It is most important that your child knows whom they may trust in an emergency. We might often tell our children that strangers cannot be trusted and emphasise the 'stranger danger' message. However, in an emergency, your child may have to allow strangers into the home. This is most likely to be emergency service providers but you might like to have discussions regarding others that you feel your child can safely trust to ask for help. Trustworthy neighbours that your child could access easily in the event of an emergency should be indicated to your child.

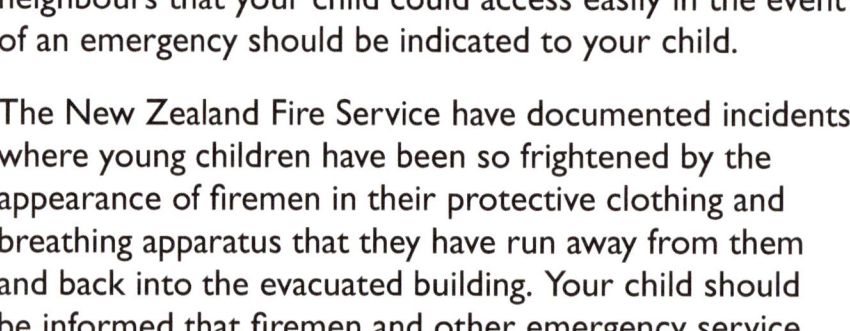

The New Zealand Fire Service have documented incidents where young children have been so frightened by the appearance of firemen in their protective clothing and breathing apparatus that they have run away from them and back into the evacuated building. Your child should be informed that firemen and other emergency service personnel may look scary but they can be trusted to help.

Suggested questions

- *Why is it important that we don't trust all strangers?*
- *Which strangers can you trust?*
- *Can you trust a fireman/policeman/ambulance person that you don't know? (You might like to inform your child that ambulance personnel may also be called paramedics.)*
- *If there was an emergency, who could you ask for help?*

Page 10 – 'Little Life Savers know where the first-aid box is kept'

Although it is vital that medicines and poisons are kept out of children's reach, it is useful to show your child the contents of the first-aid kit and its location.

Suggested questions

- *Where is our first-aid kit/box kept?*
- *Do you know what we keep in the first-aid kit/box?*
- *Do you know why we keep a first-aid kit/box?*
- *Why is it really important that you don't touch the first-aid kit/box?*

Page 11 – "Well done, Sam and Lucy. You are Little Life Savers'

Praise is a useful tool to build a child's confidence and self-belief. It can influence learning opportunities and motivate positive behaviour. Working through this resource and giving praise for correct responses should assure your child that they are very capable of staying safe in an emergency and perhaps ensuring the well-being of others, too.

Suggested questions

- *What clever things did Lucy do to help Grandma?*
- *What clever things did Sam do to help Grandma?*

Page 12 – 'Little Life Savers practise fire drills. The smoke alarm makes a loud noise but it does not frighten Lucy and Sam. Little Life Savers don't run and hide.'

Smoke alarms are loud and can frighten children into hiding in confined spaces. This response could seriously threaten the safety of your child. Once you have discussed escape routes from your home and prepared your child for the volume of the alarm, trigger the smoke alarm at regular intervals to practise safe evacuation. This practice also tests the function of the smoke alarm. All smoke alarms in the home should be checked regularly if they are not hard-wired into the electricity supply. It is recommended that batteries are changed every six months.

It is most important that your child is informed to leave the house immediately and stay out. Your child should not be tempted to go into another room or re-enter the house to call the emergency services. Instead, you can teach your child to shout the word 'fire' repeatedly. You might like to time your child to see how long it takes them to escape the house and make sure that they can follow different escape plans in less than three minutes, since fires can quickly become devastating.

Suggested questions

- *What should you do every time you hear the smoke alarm?*
- *What should you do if you don't hear the smoke alarm but can see fire or smoke (or smell smoke)?*
- *Should you escape from the house quickly even though you know it's just a practice?*
- *Why should we try to get out of the house as quickly as we can?*
- *What is the best escape route from your bedroom (etc.)?*
- *If the door is blocked, how else can you escape?*
- *Should you try to call 111 from inside your house?*
- *What should you shout if you think there is a fire or when we practise fire drill?*

Page 13 – 'Sam knows what to do if there is a real fire'

Your child should be instructed never to try to rescue anyone or anything from the house. Little Life Savers might be very tempted to rush to help a parent, sibling, pet or precious toy, but your child must be taught to save only him/herself. Little Life Savers must never be tempted to open the door of a room containing fire or smoke.

Suggested questions

- *Why do you think we should keep the door closed to the kitchen if it is on fire?*
- *When you think there is a fire, should you try to rescue anyone?*
- *When you think there is a real fire, should you rescue (name pet)?*
- *When you think there is a real fire, is it okay to save a really precious toy?*
- *Should you ever go back inside for anything?*

Page 14 – 'Lucy knows what to do if there is a real fire'

Smoke is toxic and causes more fatalities than flames. Smoke will be more concentrated high in the room so your child should be taught how to get down low and get out fast. If the smoke level is low, it may be necessary to crawl out of the house.

Suggested questions

- *What is so dangerous about smoke?*
- *Where in the room do you think most of the smoke will be?*
- *What are some of the things we can do to stay safe from smoke?*

Page 15 – 'Sam and Lucy know lots of ways to get out of their house'

Alternative escape routes should be discussed in different locations around the home and perhaps allocated a preference. Your child should practise how to escape from every room in the house. As your child becomes more confident with the fire drill, you might like to block the obvious exits to test the child's knowledge of alternative escape plans. For example, if you live in a two-storeyed home, consider a plan of action if your child is trapped upstairs. In this instance, it would be prudent to teach your child to find a room upstairs where there is no fire, close the door, open the window and shout for help.

Suggested questions

- *What do you think is the easiest way to get out of the house?*
- *What would you do if you couldn't get out of the house that (the preferred) way?*
- *If the front door and the back door are blocked, what other ways can we get out of the house?*

Page 16 – 'Little Life Savers know a safe place to wait for help'

To prepare for an emergency evacuation, a safe meeting place away from the house must be decided upon. The safe meeting spot should be far enough away from the house and power lines and close to a road or driveway. This enables emergency personnel to find your child and perhaps identify the location of the emergency more promptly. A gate or letterbox could be considered safe options when waiting for emergency services to arrive.

Suggested questions

- *Where do we meet when we practise fire drill and escaping from the house?*
- *Do you think this is a safe place to meet?*
- *Where should we meet every time we hear the smoke alarm or see fire or smoke?*
- *What can we shout when we are at the meeting place?*

Page 17 – 'We put the fire out. Lucy and Sam, you are Little Life Savers'

Little Life Savers should be reminded that their own safety is most important and that rescuing themselves is equally as heroic as rescuing others. Children can panic in emergency situations. However, it is hoped that by working through this book, your child will be adequately prepared to make safer choices to maintain personal safety. If you have any concerns that your child may be tempted to take heroic steps to rescue a pet or family member, you may wish to remind him/her that Little Life Savers who look after their own safety don't require rescuing and therefore help to keep others safe, too.

Suggested questions

- *When there was a real fire, what clever things did Lucy do?*
- *When there was a real fire, what clever things did Sam do?*
- *If there is a real fire, who is the only person you should rescue?*

Page 18 – 'Sam can feel an earthquake'

Earthquakes can be disturbing to children. To introduce this topic to your child, you could explain that an earthquake happens when two plates of the earth suddenly slip past one another. You could reassure your child that most earthquakes are too small and deep to be felt.

Suggested questions

- *What do you think an earthquake is?*
- *What does an earthquake feel like?*

Page 19 – 'Lucy knows there is an earthquake'

Most injuries during earthquakes are caused by impact from moving objects and it's important that your child is taught to respond immediately when they feel an earthquake. Your child should be told to act without waiting for instruction from you or anyone else.

Suggested questions

- *What can happen during an earthquake?*
- *Why must you find a safe place as quickly as you can?*

Page 20 – 'Little Life Savers know how to find a safe place during an earthquake'

Civil defence agencies continue to promote the 'drop, cover and hold' response to earthquakes. Preliminary research into actions taken during the Canterbury earthquakes indicates that this remains the best response. Your child should be taught to respond quickly and find a sturdy piece of furniture within a few steps that could provide protection. Or, if this is not possible, they should be told to stand close to an interior wall until the earthquake stops.

Suggested questions

- *Why do you think Sam is under his bed?*
- *Why do you think he is covering his head?*
- *Can you show me how to 'drop, cover and hold'?*

Page 21 – 'Mum and Dad know they are safe'

Homes can be made safer for your child by securing large or heavy pieces of furniture to the wall or floor. During an earthquake, the furniture your child is sheltering under may move away and expose your child to impact from other moving objects. Your child could be told to hold onto the protective shelter if it is not secured to the floor.

There are a few other things you can do with your child to be better prepared for an earthquake. You could assemble and maintain an emergency response kit for your home. You could also practise 'drop, cover and hold' drills and discuss with your child how to find other safe places around the home.

Suggested questions

- *Why do you think Lucy is under the table?*
- *Why do you think she is holding the leg of the table?*
- *What other safe places could you go to if you felt an earthquake?*

Page 22 – 'The earthquake has stopped. Lucy and Sam, you know how to stay safe'

Little Life Savers should be taught to stay in the identified safe place until the ground stops shaking and told to expect some aftershocks following a significant earthquake. Aftershocks can be big enough to continue to move objects and furniture. You may prefer to tell your child to stay in the safe place until an adult tells him/her to leave.

Suggested questions

- *How long do you think Sam and Lucy should stay in their safe places?*
- *What did Sam and Lucy do during the earthquake that was clever?*
- *What should you do if there is an earthquake at home, kindy, the supermarket, etc.?*

Page 23-24 'Lucy and Sam, you are cool Little Life Savers. You know how to stay safe. Great work'

By now, your Little Life Saver should realise that different emergencies require different responses.

It is hoped that, by reading this book regularly with your child, these responses will be learned and executed appropriately, without fear or panic, if they are ever required.

Simple information, such as the emergency number, the name of the town/city in which you live or the name of the closest crossroad may help to keep your child safe and your child's knowledge of these details should not be assumed.

It is also hoped that your child has clearly understood that it is not necessary to rescue someone in order to be a Little Life Saver. A real Little Life Saver knows how important it is to keep him/herself safe in an emergency and this could help to maintain the safety of others, too.

Suggested questions

- *Whose life did Sam save?*
- *Whose life did Lucy save?*
- *If we have an emergency, whose life will you save?*
- *Do you know all the right things to do and say?*
- *Do you know that makes you a cool Little Life Saver, too?*

The Contents of a Safe Home

In addition to educated and empowered Little Life Savers, safe homes should contain the following:

- *An evacuation plan (available from www.fire.org.nz)*
- *A household emergency plan and checklist (available from www.getthru.govt.nz)*
- *Functioning smoke alarms*
- *Unobstructed fire exits, e.g., keys in deadlocks*
- *A phone within reach*
- *Well-maintained gas and electrical appliances*
- *Torch with spare batteries or a self-charging torch*
- *Radio with spare batteries*

Wind and waterproof clothing, sun hats, and strong

- *First-aid kit*
- *Emergency survival items*
- *Fire extinguisher*
- *Fire blanket*
- *Garden hose attached to a tap*
- *A house number that's clearly visible from the road*
- *Furnishings and clothing kept at least 1 metre away from heat sources*

First-aid Kit Suggested Contents

First-aid kits may be purchased from St John, your local pharmacy or you can make your own.

- *First-aid kit*
- *Triangular bandage*
- *Roller bandages*
- *Sterile gauze - 7.5 x 7.5 (2)*
- *Adhesive wound dressing*
- *Plaster strip dressings*
- *Adhesive tape - 25mm hypoallergenic*
- *Sterile non-adhesive pads*
- *Sterile eye pad*
- *Eye wash container*
- *Eye wash solution*
- *Antiseptic solution*
- *Safety pins*
- *Scissors*
- *Tweezers*
- *Disposable gloves*
- *Accident register and pencil*
- *First-aid manual*
- *Card listing local emergency numbers*

Emergency Response Kit

- Torch with spare batteries or a self-charging torch
- Radio with spare batteries
- Wind and waterproof clothing, sun hats and strong outdoor shoes.
- First-aid kit and essential medicines
- Blankets or sleeping bags
- Pet supplies
- Toilet paper and large rubbish bags for your emergency toilet
- Face and dust masks
- Non-perishable food (canned or dried food)
- Food, formula and drinks for babies and small children
- Water for drinking (at least 3 litres per person, per day)
- Water for washing and cooking
- A primus or gas barbeque to cook on
- A can opener
- Make sure you have plenty of petrol in your car

Getaway Kit

In some emergencies you may need to evacuate quickly. Everyone should have a packed getaway kit in an easily accessible place at home which includes:

- Torch and radio with spare batteries
- Any special needs items such as hearing aids, glasses or mobility aids
- Emergency water and easy-to-carry food rations such as energy bars, dried foods and any special dietary requirements
- First-aid kit and essential medicines
- Essential items for infants or young children such as formula and food, nappies and a favourite toy
- Change of clothes (wind/waterproof clothing and strong outdoor shoes)
- Toiletries – towel, soap, toothbrush, sanitary items, toilet paper
- Food and water for at least 3 days
- Blankets or sleeping bags
- Face and dust masks
- Pet supplies
- Important documents: identification (birth & marriage certificates, driver's licence, passports), financial documents (e.g. insurance policies and mortgage information), and precious family photos

This information was obtained from www.getthru.govt.nz. For more information and activities on staying safe around the home, emergency response and preparedness, visit:

www.getfirewise.org.nz
www.fire.org.nz
www.getthru.govt.nz
www.homesafety.co.nz

www.police.govt.nz/safety
www.youth.stjohn.org.nz
www.eq-iq.org.nz

About Stella McCallum

Stella McCallum has worked as a nurse in Scotland, England, Australia and New Zealand. Post Graduate study led to a career change into occupational health nursing, and industrial health and safety. As a parent of twin boys she was frustrated at the lack of resources available for teaching pre-schoolers how to stay safe. From this frustration came *Little Life Savers at Home*, the first in a series of safety books for under-fives. This project encompasses Stella's passion for safety education and writing itself.

About Alan and Dennis Poole

Alan and Dennis Poole are illustrators, currently living on the Kapiti Coast, Wellington, New Zealand. Their work has predominantly been in the education sector, where they have worked for a variety of New Zealand publishers. They continually strive to produce illustrations that are vibrant, informative, and accurate.

Tangerine
appeeling books

If you enjoyed *Little Life Savers at Home*, please support us by visiting and registering with the following sites and leaving great feedback:

www.amazon.com
www.goodreads.com

and like www.tangerinepublications.com on Facebook
You can visit our website at www.tangerinepublications.com
Your support is appreciated and will help small independent publishers like us bring you more great titles.

First published by Tangerine Publications 2013
Published by Tangerine Publications Ltd
www.tangerinepublications.com
PO Box 4135
Whanganui, 4541
New Zealand

Text Copyright © 2013 Stella McCallum
Illustrations Copyright © 2013 Alan and Dennis Poole
Design: Penny Richardson www.jellyfishcreative.co.nz
Printed by H & A Print, Whanganui
The author and illustrators assert their moral rights.

All rights reserved.
ISBN 978-0-987-66467-9

This book or electronic equivalent is sold subject to the condition that it shall not, by way of trade or otherwise, be lent, hired out or otherwise circulated in any form, format or cover other than that in which it is published. No part of this publication may be reproduced, stored in a retrieval system, or transmitted in any form or by any means (electronic, mechanical, photocopying, recording or otherwise) without prior permission of the publisher.

www.ingramcontent.com/pod-product-compliance
Lightning Source LLC
LaVergne TN
LVHW071026070426
835507LV00002B/46